S0-ACB-232

BETTER EDUCATION *Through* BULLETIN BOARDS

Written and Illustrated by
Helen L. Horne

Exposition Press New York

EXPOSITION PRESS INC.

50 Jericho Turnpike Jericho, New York 11753

FIRST EDITION

0-682-47289-1

ACKNOWLEDGMENTS

Better Education Through Bulletin Boards has become a reality because of people to whom I am indebted far greater than I can ever repay. These people have played a particularly important part in my development as an individual, and consequently, *Better Education Through Bulletin Boards* has become more than notes written on 3x5 cards. I owe and give special thanks first, to my parents for their continued guidance, love and encouragement in all my endeavors; then to Mrs. Helen N. Cook who has always exemplified the highest and noblest ideals of the teaching profession through her instruction and example. Grateful appreciation is expressed to Mr. Frances Couch, Chairman of the Commercial Art Department of Muriel Dobbins Vocational High School in Philadelphia, who graciously consented to sketch the original drawings for the book. Finally, and most of all, to the children themselves, who inspired me to provide for them an extension of their education through the use of creative and original bulletin board materials.

Contents

Introduction

Today, more than ever, children are captured by the visual presentation of materials and ideas. A bulletin board attractively decorated that conveys a meaningful message can perhaps be the vehicle that will motivate and encourage youngsters to improve their overall school performance. An idea presented on a bulletin board could very well relate to a youngster's area of interest and thereby provide an avenue through which the teacher can involve the youngster in a wider range of classroom activities.

Many teachers consider a bulletin board to be a display that remains up for a month and indicates to anyone visiting the classroom what kinds of things are being taught and perhaps how. This is true, but bulletin boards can also be of a manipulative nature and can be used to prepare youngsters for a given lesson. Manipulative objects can be used quite easily in the area of mathematics.

The ideas presented in this book are intended as suggestions and do not have to be displayed exactly as indicated. It is hoped that you will use your own individuality and creativity to develop and change these ideas further. Also, remember that your students themselves can create very interesting boards and enjoy putting up the display. You should also be aware of the materials and objects that can be found in our everyday environment. Such things as decorated facial tissue, brightly colored yarn, and decorated paper wrappings can be used for lettering and background.

All ideas presented in this book are the author's original ideas, and any resemblance to other bulletin board materials is purely coincidental.

WELCOME
to room 13
JACK
SYBIL
SUE
HELEN
MARY
RICK
BEN
AL
JAY
MAE
BEA
JOE
LOU

September

Begin the school year with a timely design. The school can be drawn with a felt-tip pen, or you may use a picture of the school. The footprints may be of different colors—white for girls and gray for boys or vice versa. The letters may be cut from pink and white construction paper. A red background would blend well with the design.

This board will help you begin the new school year with a fall theme. The tree trunk and branches may be cut from brown construction paper. The leaves may be of different colors or the same color. Each leaf should have the name of a different student printed on it. Letters can be cut from black construction paper. A background of orange or another contrasting color would blend well. The children may come to the board and find their names.

LET OUR TREE
GROW
AS WE
LEARN
ANN
JOE
JIM
ED
MARY
KAY
BOB
SUE
JUNE
JACK
NAT
TED
DOT

WELCOME
BACK
TO
SCHOOL
JEAN
GEORGE
CHARLES
HELEN
NAOMI
JOE
FRANK
FANNY
SAM
SYBIL
JOHN

This board can serve a dual purpose. It can be used to decorate the classroom and to extend to youngsters a personal welcome back to school. Red and black silhouettes are used in this design. Place red silhouettes on top of black so as to give a shadowed effect. Silhouettes are surrounded by twisted orange crylon or a similar type yarn. Each silhouette may have the name of a different student printed on it. Letters may be cut from red or black construction paper, and the background may be white or another contrasting color. Children may come to the board and point to the silhouette which has their name on it.

October

A Halloween warning is noted in this bulletin board. A background of orange would lend itself well to the contrasting white and black ghost and witch. The lettering can be white, except for the word "Halloween," which should be black. The word "spooky" should be scalloped for a realistic effect.

HAVE A
SPOOKY
BUT SAFE
HALLOWEEN

Our BEST On BOARD

This board can double as a good work board and observance of Columbus' discovery of America. The background can be yellow and each ship a different color: red, white, and blue. Outline the waves in powder blue. The lettering can be black or some other contrasting color.

OCTOBER ACROSTIC

Columbus sailed the ocean blue in 1492.
On and on he went till his men were few.
Land he spied—oh, yes, 'tis true.
Up on the land their anchors they threw—
Men of strength, of courage few.
But on he pushed his helping crew,
Until no distant land he knew.
Sail no more—his flag he flew.

This is an acrostic that tells of Columbus' voyage to America. It could be used during an October assembly celebrating the discovery of America. Each youngster should hold one of the letters of Columbus' name, and the accompanying line of verse could be printed on the back of each letter and read by each child. Back each letter with construction paper.

November

This board lends itself well as a decorative board in observance of Thanksgiving and as a display board for good work. The background can be alternating colors of orange and brown construction paper. The letters can be white and should be cut freehand to give emphasis. Pictures of turkeys and Pilgrims may be placed at the bottom of the board as decoration when no good work papers are displayed on the board.

SOMETHING TO
GOBBLE
ABOUT

This bulletin board has a theme of Thanksgiving as illustrated in the cornucopia and Constitution. The background can be orange, and the cornucopia can be brown or gray. A variety of fruits and vegetables can be placed at the opening. The Constitution should be white or yellow. The lettering can be black and white.

WE GIVE THANKS for

CONSTITUTION

MANY THINGS

ST. NICK SEES

OUR BEST

December

This board lends itself well as a decorative board for Christmas, as well as a display board for good work. The border should be green, extending almost to the center of the board, which should have a white center. St. Nick's head should be of red construction paper with features outlined in white chalk. Lettering can be black or white.

This board has a Christmas theme and can serve as a reminder to pupils to be prepared for school. The background can be white with a red border. The tree should be green and the lettering can be red. The school supplies can be of assorted colors.

DECORATE Your

TREE WITH

GIFTS of SUCCESS

January

This board might be used to activa
motivated youngsters. Any contrasting
background for this huge leaf, which sh
struction paper. One of the smaller leave
the other should be outlined only, in ord
The lettering should be red and black.

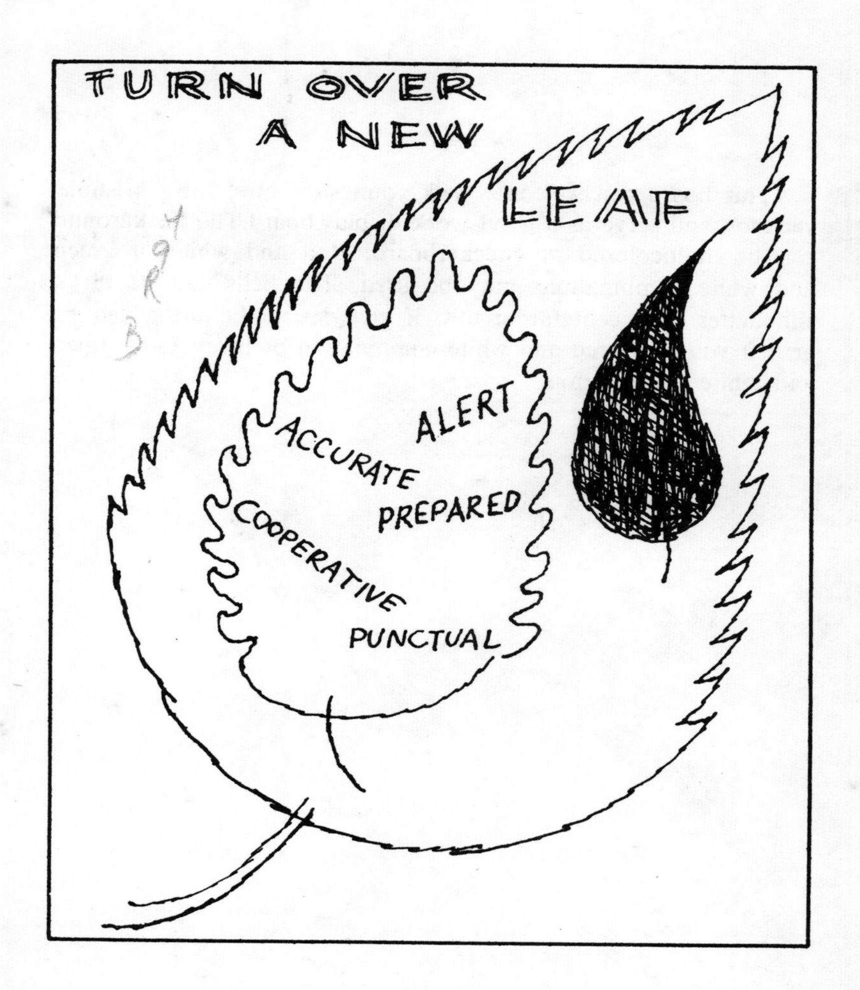
TURN OVER
A NEW
LEAF
ALERT
ACCURATE
PREPARED
COOPERATIVE
PUNCTUAL

This board can welcome back youngsters after the Christmas vacation and serve as a good work display board. The background can be multicolored or checkerboard. Red and white or green and white combinations may be used. The bells can be black silhouettes with centers cut out, if you desire. Lettering can be gray if you use a red and white combination or black for a green and white combination.

BEST
FOR 19

LOVE
YOUR
COUNTRY
AND
YOUR
FELLOWMAN
AS
DID
YOUR
FOREFATHERS

February

Red, white, and blue are the colors for this bulletin board. The background should be white to give the needed contrast to the red valentines. Silhouettes of Washington and Lincoln would be effective if done in black. The lettering on the valentines can be done freehand with a felt-tip pen.

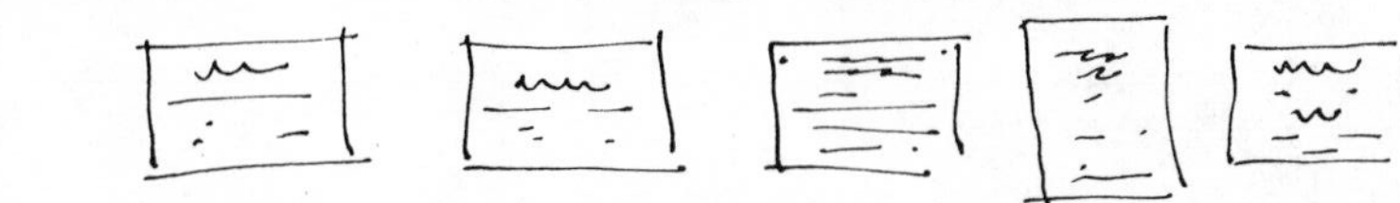

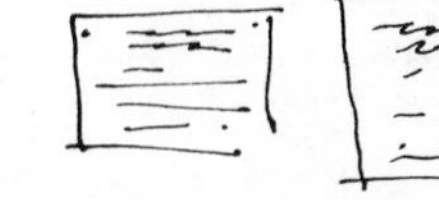

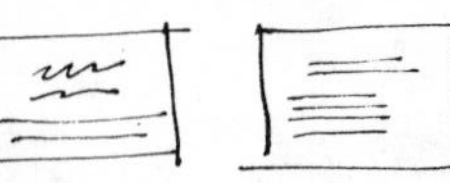

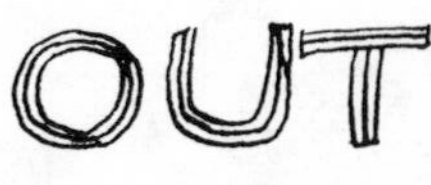
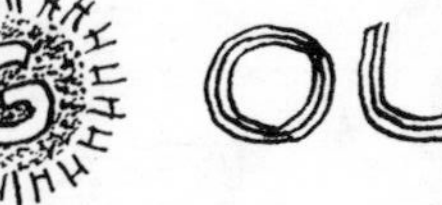

MARCH
LET YOUR BEST
SPRING OUT

March

This board doubles as a "good work" display board and a decorative board to welcome in spring. The background can be yellow or orange. Lettering can be of black construction paper. Assorted colors of construction paper can be stapled to the board and pupils' papers placed on top of each sheet, allowing part of the construction paper to show. Flowers can be of various colors. Print the word "spring" on flowers with a felt-tip pen.

April

The images of spring can be displayed with this board. A white background with blue lettering would be a good contrast. Raindrops can be cut from light blue construction paper and pictures drawn in them with a felt-tip pen. The clouds could be constructed in outline using blue yarn. The flowers can be cut from paper of many bright colors.

APRIL
SHOWERS
BRING

May

This is a board that pays tribute to Mother. The background could be pink and the lettering of a contrasting color. You could draw a picture of Mother or cut out a picture and staple it to the board. The flowers can be of many bright colors. The words on the flowers can be printed with black felt-tip pen. The stems of all the flowers could be made of brightly colored yarn.

is for *mornings* of cheer and delight.

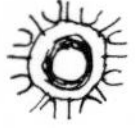

is for *opening* our minds for knowledge and light.

is for *telling* us not to start a fight.

is for *helping* us with $a + 4 = 6$, which proved to be right.

is for *each* bit of guidance that showed us the light.

is for *remembering* to kiss us good night.

This acrostic could be used as a verse on a Mother's Day card or as part of a bulletin board in the classroom. The background could be yellow and the flowers of different contrasting colors. The letters could be printed with felt-tip pens to match the colors of the flowers.

June

This board will remind children of safe summer play. The background can be yellow and the lettering black. You can display pictures of safe summer sports and activities.

HAVE
FUN
BUT
BE
SAFE

This June board will serve as a review of the math you've taught during the year. The background can be of red construction paper. The train can be white, while the letters are black and the numbers yellow. The triangles with numbers can be of contrasting colors. The lettering can be black and done freehand.

We've Taken A LONG Ride
NEW
MATH
TRAIN
□△○
2+□+△=8
3+4=□
□-5=5
8<12
□+5=7
6<9
3+5=6+2

Black History

This board can serve a dual purpose. It can be displayed in observance of Dr. Martin Luther King's birthday, and also for the observance of Brotherhood Week. The background can be blue. Four silhouettes should be cut to represent the children. Use black, white, red, and yellow—one silhouette of each color. Dr. King's portrait should be backed by paper of a contrasting color. The lettering can be yellow or white.

Fulfill His Dream Of

TOLERANCE

LOVE

UNDERSTANDING

GOODWILL

January 15, 1929 - April 4, 1968

BROTHERHOOD

MARTIN LUTHER KING

Martin Luther King—his spirit shall live on.
All his dreams and hopes shall this nation spawn,
Rights of men that have been withdrawn,
Thrusting evil upon all the wrongs.
In time we shall see if he died in vain.
Nothing shall soothe the hurt we know until full equality is gained.

Lynching and terror will no longer reign
Upon the mountaintop or down in the plain.
Thirty-nine years he searched for his peoples' gain.
Hear, America, as he speaks from his grave,
Expressing the love for his fellow man he so freely gave.
Remember when he walked the streets of Memphis, with hatred paved.

Kisses of death before him they laid.
In stubborn silence they passed and gazed.
None would dare look or his conscience ask.
Gone is Martin, but "FREE AT LAST!"

This is an acrostic that tells of Dr. King's death. It could be used during a January assembly celebrating his birthday. Each youngster should hold one of the letters of Dr. King's name, and the accompanying line of verse could be printed on the back of each letter and read by each child. The letters should be backed by construction paper of a contrasting color.

This board could be used during the months of January and February because it represents the ideals and life styles of January and February greats. The background can be of red construction paper. The tombstones can be gray. The treasure chest can be white. The lettering can be black. You may use a felt-tip pen for the tombstone lettering.

HAVE YOU
BURIED
IT??
PREJUDICE
HATRED
ENVY
INTOLERANCE
DISRESPECT

Math

This is a manipulative board that can be used to review ordinal numbers with first graders. On the right-hand side of the board tack six silhouettes of children of varying heights. Members of the class will put them in order according to height. For background, blue or red construction paper could be used. The silhouettes can be white or black. The lettering should be of a contrasting color.

WHO SHOULD BE
FIRST SECOND THIRD FOURTH FIFTH SIXTH
1 2 3 4 5 6

These number faces can be used to review number recognition with a first grade class. The background can be any color that will contrast with the colors of the faces. Use bright colors of red, orange, and blue. Faces should be outlined.

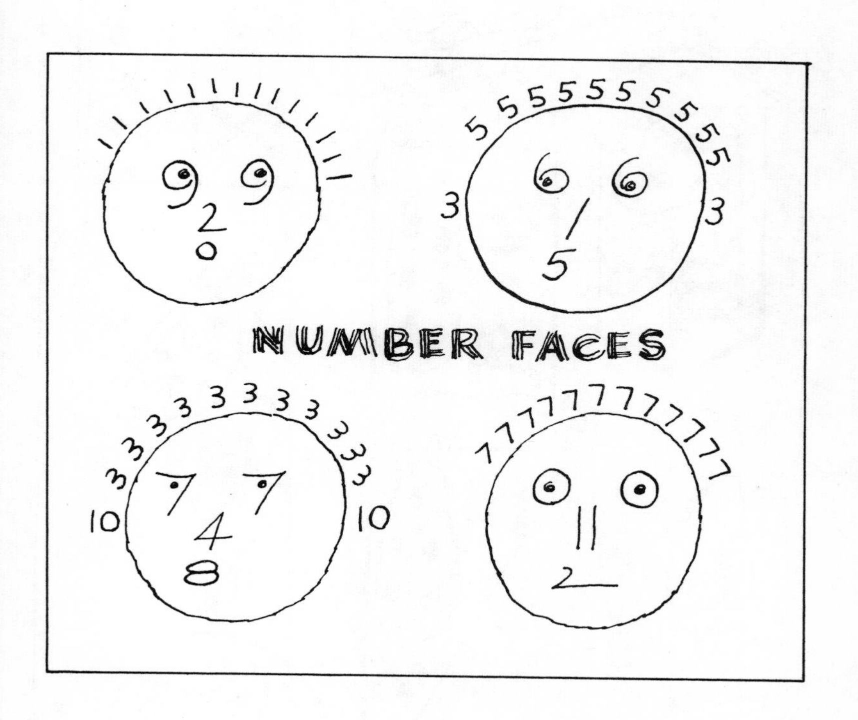
NUMBER FACES

1 I
II 2
III 3
IV 4
V 5
VI 6
VII 7
VIII 8
IX 9
X 10

This bulletin board can be used as a permanent review of numbers for a first grade class. It can remain up for a long period of time. The roman numerals should be cut from newspaper. The background can be red. The numbers and geometric shapes can be of contrasting colors of construction paper.

Science

This board can be used to stimulate interest in math and science at the same time. It is based upon the "greater than—less than" principle. Divide the board into two parts. The background can be of red construction paper. The large caption letters should be white, and the smaller letters can be black. The numbers can be yellow. For comparisons on the science side, one piece of paper (left side) *must* be gray and the other (right side) *must* be a piece of aluminum foil. The paper in the middle should be pink.

SCIENCE ACROSTIC

See if there is a problem.
Come to a conclusion.
Inspect the organism or object.
Examine its details.
Note our investigation.
Consider it carefully.
Enter findings in our notebook.

This board, while not primarily decorative, can add to the classroom environment if appropriate colors are used. This is a science acrostic that tells of the scientific approach. Any brightly colored background and letters of a contrasting color may be used. You might also print the words with a felt-tip pen.

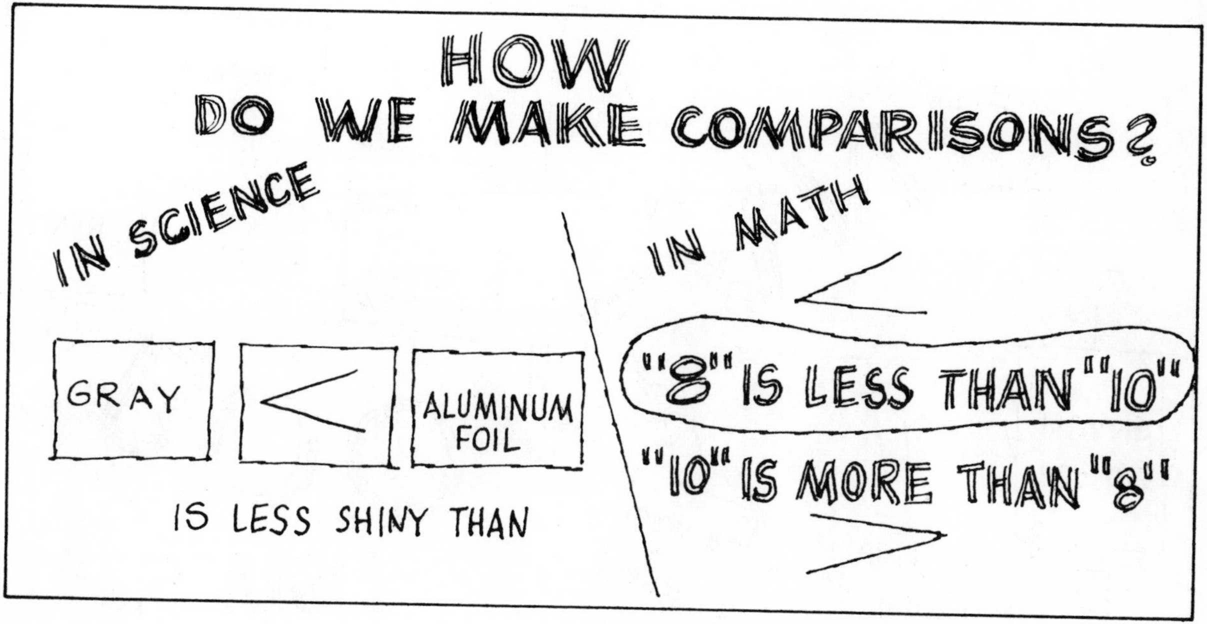

HOW DO WE MAKE COMPARISONS?

IN SCIENCE

GRAY < ALUMINUM FOIL

IS LESS SHINY THAN

IN MATH

<

"8" IS LESS THAN "10"

"10" IS MORE THAN "8"

>

LET'S VISIT
BOOKLAND
HANSEL and GRETEL
HARRIET TUBMAN
TREASURE ISLAND
ANANSI
ALICE'S ADVENTURES IN WONDERLAND
MARTIN LUTHER KING'S BOYHOOD
MALCOLM X

Books

This bulletin board can be used to stimulate interest in reading. The background can be of yellow construction paper. The book covers should be of different colors. The titles on each book can be written with a felt-tip pen. The lettering for the board can be black and red.

This is a bulletin board that will encourage your students to do more reading. The background can be blue or red. The book jackets can be any contrasting color. Parts of an actual newspaper would be very effective. The lettering should be cut from newspaper or some contrasting color of construction paper.

BE NEWSY
MAGAZINES
READ
NEWSPAPERS
BOOKS
FIND OUT:
WHO-WHAT-WHEN
WHERE-WHY ???

"IF I COULD TALK I WOULD SAY..."
PROTECT ME FROM WATER
DON'T BEND THE ENDS OF MY PAGES
WASH HANDS BEFORE READING ME
DON'T LEAVE PENCILS BETWEEN MY PAGES
KEEP ME COVERED AT ALL TIMES
READ ME OFTEN

This board could be displayed in your reading corner to remind children of proper book care. Any contrasting color can be used as background for the huge book, which should be of red construction paper. The smaller book jackets can be actual book jackets or assorted colors of construction paper. The lettering on each book cover can be done with a black felt-tip pen. The large lettering can be yellow and white.

Manners

If your youngsters appear to be forgetting their manners, this board will remind them. The background can be blue, and the doors can be yellow or orange. The letters can be any contrasting color.

GOOD MANNERS OPEN

THANK YOU

EXCUSE ME

PLEASE

NO THANK YOU

MAY I

THE DOORS TO FRIENDSHIPS

GOOD MANNERS
WIN FRIENDS

This board can serve as a reminder to youngsters that good manners and friendship go hand in hand. If placed on a bulletin board that is visible to the entire class, this board can remain up for a long period of time. A brown background should be used because it will not show fading as quickly as brighter colors. An appropriate picture that you may have in your picture file may be displayed. Lettering can be white and orange.

Tips and Ideas to Put Fun In Learning

LANGUAGE ARTS

Spelling

If your children are having difficulty with spelling, you can improve their ability to spell through the use of typewriters. You can secure used typewriters from dealers who will be happy to donate them to your school if you tell them the purpose for which they are going to be used. Another way is to purchase "toy" typewriters from the store (those that use typewriter ribbons). These typewriters can be purchased for as little as $7.00, and could be a very worthwhile investment because they could be used in connection with other subjects. Your class might consider a pretzel sale or cake sale in order to raise enough money for the purchase of these typewriters.

Once you have secured your typewriters, you could have your children work in small groups with one of the students dictating sentences using spelling words and the children typing them as they are called. If you are fortunate enough to have a classroom aide, perhaps she can assist in this way.

Alphabet Faces

The alphabet faces on the opposite page can be used to review the alphabet with a first grade class. Use any contrasting colors.

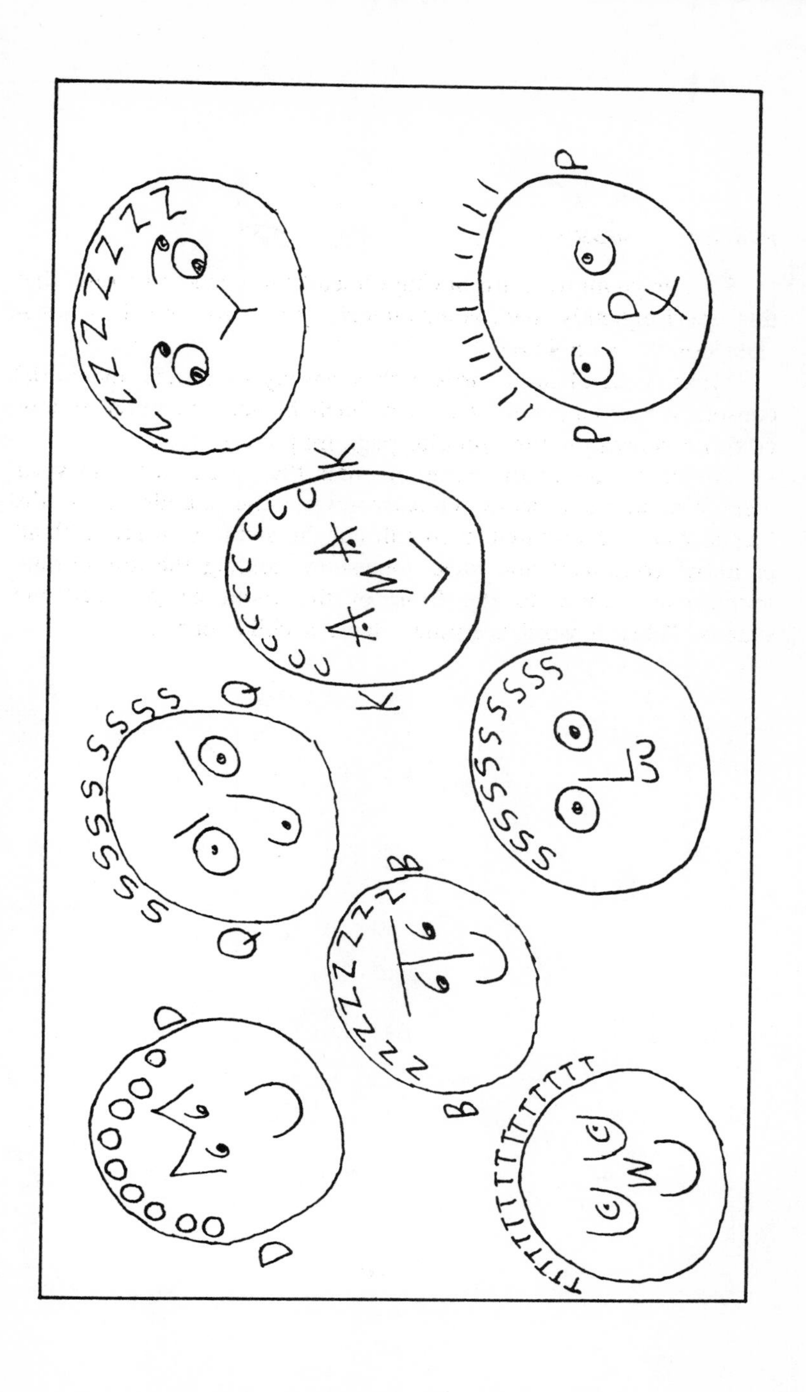

Phonics

If your youngsters are having difficulty in decoding words that they see frequently, here is an interesting way to help them associate sounds with letters.

Make a set of flash cards with a variety of blends and initial consonant sounds printed on them. Such blends and initial sounds as those shown on the opposite page may be used.

Attach strings to the cards in order that youngsters can wear them around their necks. Quickly review the sounds of all the blends you've distributed, then call out the sound of a given blend or initial consonant and have youngsters holding the appropriate sound cards come to the front of the room as you call the sounds. When a word is formed, have a child read it.

br
qu
ch
sh
m
p
n

Reading

This is a good way to develop youngsters' sight vocabulary and letter recognition.

Give each child a magazine or an outdated textbook. Have him cut out words and make short sentences. The words can be pasted onto a large sheet of paper. You might ask the children to construct sentences using color words, number words, and shape words. This would depend upon the kinds of words your children are most likely to find in the books or magazines they use.

MATHEMATICS

Number Cards

In order to review mathematical facts, you can prepare a set of numeral cards, 0–9, using manila oak tag. Cut out squares 2½″x3″ and write one number on each card. Each youngster should have a set of cards to keep in his desk. You can hold up number facts flash cards and have the children hold up the card which shows the answer.

The number cards could be used for addition, subtraction, multiplication, and division.

Answer Cards

Another way of reviewing mathematical facts would be through the use of manila oak tag answer cards. These can be made by cutting a piece of oak tag to 5″x8″ size and dividing it into four columns, each column 2½″ wide. At the top of each column you write a number. Then cut out sixteen small rectangles 1″x2½″. On these rectangles you can write various number facts.

The youngster places the small number fact card in the column that shows the answer to that number fact.

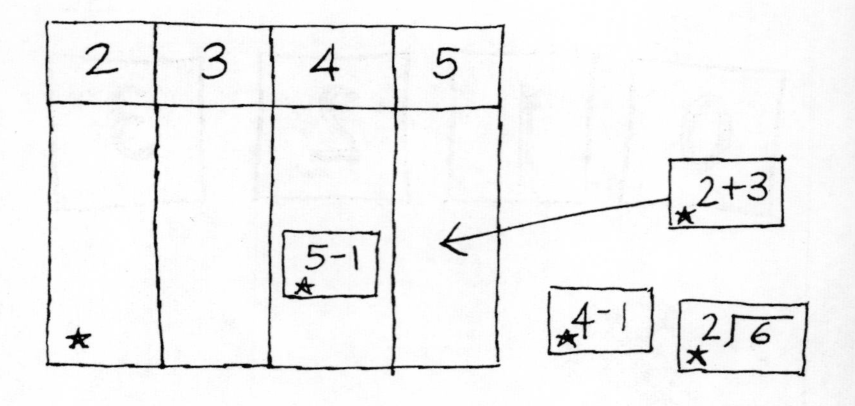

These cards can be used for addition, subtraction, multiplication, and division.

Your answer cards may be placed in a box as part of your "leisure time" activities or remain with youngsters at their desks. These can be used independently by children after they have completed their assigned classwork.

You might find it helpful to code each set of answer cards in the event pieces fall out or become mixed up with another students cards. Coding could be in the form of a small green or blue star in the corner of each piece or a red square, etc.

When not in use, the small cards can be inserted in a pocket attached to the back of the card.

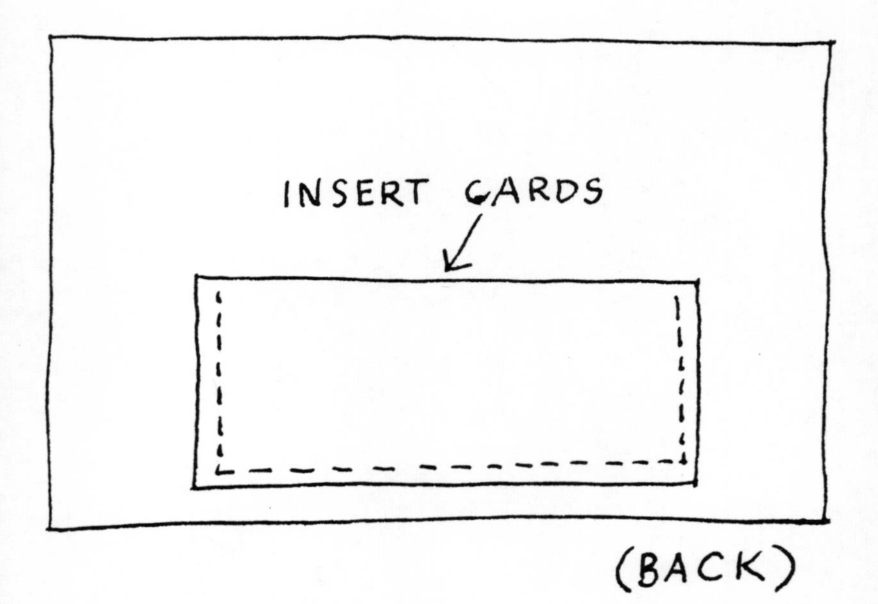